Aloha Tower Market Place

The Aloha Tower was built in 1926 as a symbol of the Hawaiian Islands, to be remembered by the ships entering and leaving Honolulu Harbor. For four decades it stood as the tallest building in Hawai'i, and though today even higher structures are visible in downtown Honolulu, the surrounding land boasts a popular open-air marketplace with shops and restaurants. Cruise ships appear to be parked on a Honolulu street when tied up in port.

Downtown Honolulu

Downtown Honolulu: Honolulu is the largest city in the Islands, and its bustling downtown is home to diverse local and national businesses. Bordering the modern high rises is the historic residence of the Hawaiian monarchy, 'Iolani Palace, as well as the current seat of state government, Honolulu Hale.

ʻIolani Palace

King Kalākaua's ornate ʻIolani Palace, completed in 1882, was the royal residence until 1893 when the last Hawaiian monarch, Queen Liliʻuokalani was overthrown. As the Executive Building, the former palace was home to the Governor and Legislature from 1900 until the new Hawaiʻi State Capitol was dedicated in 1969.

Nuʻuanu Pali Lookout

The Nuʻuanu Pali Lookout offers superior views of Kāneʻohe, Kailua, and the Koʻolau Mountains. As the site of the last battle in 1810 to unite all the islands under Kamehameha the Great, visitors can learn about the history of Oʻahu and its growth into Hawaiʻi's most populated island.

Magic Island

This thirty-acre peninsula of Ala Moana Beach Park near Waikīkī is known as Magic Island, a popular recreational area for both visitors and residents. Picnicking, jogging, swimming, diving, and biking are all activities to be enjoyed along this "Land from the Sea."

Punchbowl Cemetery

In ancient times, the extinct Pūowaina Crater, meaning "Hill of Sacrifices" in Hawaiian, was the site of secret ali'i, or high chief, burials. It now houses the National Memorial Cemetery of the Pacific, dedicated in 1949 to those who gave their lives in military service.

Waikīkī

Built in 1927, the coral-colored Royal Hawaiian Hotel is an unmistakable presence amidst the populated Waikīkī shoreline. Once home to residences of Hawai'i's monarchy, Waikīkī Beach now offers visitors a long stretch of sea and sand with a spectacular view of the iconic Diamond Head.

Waikīkī

The southern coast of Oʻahu shows Waikīkī today through a fisheye lense from which densely built residential neighborhoods spread up towards the Koʻolau Mountain Range. In early Hawaiʻi, instead of endless buildings, one would see endless taro farms, rice fields, duck ponds, swamps, clusters of coconut trees behind an empty beach, a scattering of residences and weekend bungalows.

Diamond Head Crater

Diamond Head is Hawai'i's most famous natural landmark, inspiring voyagers, artists, poets, songwriters, naturalists, hikers, and tourism publicists. Lē'ahi, "brow of the yellowfin tuna" to the Hawaiians, was once speckled with calcite crystals mistaken by early sailors for diamonds. The 200,000-year old cone remnant looms 760 feet over Waikīkī.

Hanauma Bay

The distinct crescent of the Hanauma Bay Nature Park was formed when the ocean made its home between the two surrounding volcanic craters. Today it is one of O'ahu's most popular areas for snorkeling and swimming, and its large coral reef is a haven for colorful sea life.

Makapuʻu Lighthouse

Perched atop the black lava rock cliff of Oʻahu's most eastern point, Makapuʻu Lighthouse offers a spectacular view of the southeast shore from Rabbit and Bird Islands nearby to Waimānalo Bay. During migration season, usually November through April, whales can be spotted from the lookout.

Sea Life Park

Nestled on a small peninsula between the dramatic backdrop of the Koʻolau Mountains and the rush of the Pacific, dolphins, sea lions, and penguins perform at Sea Life Park, an educational marine attraction on Oʻahu's southeast shore.

Waimānalo Beach

One of the longest white sand beaches on Oʻahu, Waimānalo Beach is a popular family destination for town and island residents. Its small shorebreak is ideal for bodysurfing, bodyboarding, and fishing.

Mokulua Islands

The twin Mokulua Islands (from Lua—two and Moku—island) rise up from the sea just a mile offshore of the secluded community of Lanikai. A protected bird sanctuary, the islands' tidal beaches are also visited by respectful surfers and kayakers.

Mount Olomana

Sometimes referred to as Hawai'i's "Matterhorn," the twin peaks of Mount Olomana on O'ahu's windward side rise 1600 feet sharply into the sky. Located in the residential town of Maunawili, the lone remain of Ko'olau Caldera can be seen from Waimānalo to Kāne'ohe.

Coconut Island

Before it was featured in the opening scenes of Gilligan's Island, Moku O Loʻe, commonly known as Coconut Island, was originally used by shepherds and local fishermen. Today, the University of Hawaiʻi has established a marine laboratory on the sandy shores in the middle of Kāneʻohe Bay.

Kāneʻohe Bay

The protected waters of Kāneʻohe Bay are favored by sailors and windsurfers. It is the largest sheltered body of water in Hawaiʻi, and features the island chain's only barrier reef.

Lanikai

Lanikai is a small, close-knit residential community on Oʻahu's southeast shore. Its public beach is used almost exclusively by residents, and protected by a large outer reef, waves merely lap at the brilliant white shoreline.

Chinaman's Hat

The shape of this small island just offshore of Kualoa has given it the popular name of Chinaman's Hat. Its ancient name is Mokoli'i, after a giant lizard who was said to be defeated here by Hi'iaka, the sister of Pele, goddess of volcanoes.

Ka'a'awa Valley

The backdrop of many popular Hollywood films, including Jurrassic Park, the thousand acres of Ka'a'awa valley are carpeted with lush pasture land owned by Kualoa Ranch. This ancient land bordered by some of O'ahu's most formidable mountain peaks was once a sacred area of refuge.

Polynesian Cultural Center

The Mormon Temple, established in the early 1900s, sits against the backdrop of the Koʻolau Mountains, reflecting crisp blue skies in its pool. PHOTO COURTESY OF THE POLYNESIAN CULTURAL CENTER

Mālaekahana Bay

Yet another of Oʻahu's uninhabited offshore lava rock formations is Mokuʻauia, or Goat Island. Three beaches frame the shores of this twelve-acre limestone island in idyllic Mālaekahana Bay.

Turtle Bay

Just forty-five minutes from the vibrant energy of Honolulu, on the lands of Kuilima in Kahuku on the North Shore, lies the quiet luxury of the Turtle Bay Resort. The first-class but relatively isolated resort (forty miles from downtown Honolulu) is a self-contained world where guests swim, sunbathe, golf, play tennis, ride or simply escape the crowds of Waikīkī, as their whims decide.

Waimea Bay

Waimea Bay is known for huge surfing waves that annually challenge world champions. The landmark Saints Peter and Paul Mission at the base of Pūpūkea plateau originally was the tower of a rock-crushing plant build in 1928 when the Waimea-Kahuku stretch of island-circling Kamehameha Highway was paved.

U.S.S. *Arizona* Memorial

The ghostly outline of the U.S.S. *Arizona* is visible beneath the 184-foot memorial for the 1,100 crew members who perished when the battleship was sunk on the morning of December 7, 1941. Fifty years later drops of oil from her fuel tanks—filled to the brim just before the attack—rise as silent reminders of the gallant men below.

Dole Pineapple Plantation

The Pineapple Garden Maze at the Dole Plantation was named in the 2001 Guinness Book of World Records as the largest in the world. First opened as a fruit stand in 1950, the Plantation now sees nearly one-million visitors a year.

Ka'ena Point

Rugged Ka'ena Point, a natural area preserve, is the northernmost tip of O'ahu. A 2.7 mile trail along the coast follows an old railroad bed and offers dramatic views of Mākua and the Wai'anae Coast.

Wai‘anae Coast

Geographically separate from O‘ahu's city life, the Wai‘anae coast retains its naturally stunning landscape. Wide white sand beaches line the largely undeveloped valley braced against the majestic mountains that frame small agricultural communities.

Kolekole Pass

Kolekole Pass: In 1937 Army Engineers constructed a road through the deep cut in the Wai'anae Mountains knows as Kolekole Pass. Hawaiian legend connects the pass with a large stone there said to be a territorial marker or a tool in the rituals of defeated chiefs.

Ko ʻOlina

Tranquil lagoons at the Ko ʻOlina Resort and Marina hug this West Oʻahu shoreline. Hawaiian Spinner Dolphins often frequent the warm waters of this wide stretch of sea.

Tripler Hospital

Straddling Maunalani Ridge, fourteen-story 1,500-bed U.S. Army Tripler General Hospital was built when Pearl Harbor made the need for a major military hospital to serve the Pacific obvious. Only 300 hospital beds were available in 1941. One mystery remains, however: Why was Tripler Hospital painted pink?